AF225435

RETIREMENT

Sucks!

By
Mike Turnbull

Retirement Sucks! Copyright © 2019 by Mike Turnbull
Rivershore Books
Cover design by Rivershore Books
Cover photo by
Author photo courtesy of author

The opinions expressed in this manuscript are solely the opinions of the author and do not represent the opinions or thoughts of the publisher. The author represents and warrants that s/he either owns or has the legal right to publish all material in this book.

ISBN: 978-1-63522-006-3
First published in 2019

All Rights Reserved. This book may not be reproduced, transmitted, or stored in whole or in part by any means, including graphic, electronic, or mechanical without the express written consent of the publisher except in the case of brief quotations embodied in critical articles and reviews.

PRINTED IN THE UNITED STATES OF AMERICA

DEDICATION

"Retirement Sucks!" is dedicated to my family, friends, and ex-colleagues for putting up with me while I make the adjustment to this new phase of my life. Thanks for your patience, words of advice, and support. Special thanks to anyone who may have done recommendations for me when I applied for jobs.

I was a teacher and coach for the past 36 years and I felt I did a pretty good job of it. I have been retired for a few months, and I admit I am not very good at it. I am working on it and—again—thank you for helping me along this uncharted path. I really don't know where it is going, but I will try to enjoy the ride.

PREFACE

Last spring [2017] I had my fifth book published, titled "I Still Own a Flip Phone." Admittedly not my best work. I've been told by some that the format was difficult to follow. Also, some of the content upset some readers and may have cost me a couple of friendships. I feel bad about that, because that definitely was not intended.

I haven't sat down to write since then, but I have been pondering subject material. I officially retired on May 15, 2017. I had been a teacher and a coach for 36 years. I have spent the past four months coming to grips with this new phase in my life and I am already tiring of the question: "So how do you like retirement?"

To be honest, for the most part, I am not enjoying it. Thus the subject of this book.

"Retirement Sucks!"
September 21, 2017

CHAPTER ONE

THE DETAILS

I first started contemplating retirement about 8 years ago. I knew that I would reach the rule of 90 in 2015. The rule of 90, simply put, is when your age and years of service add up to 90. For me that would be 56 + 34. Not that I was hell-bent on retiring at that time, but that was when I would first be eligible.

I was the head coach for three sports for 20+ years of my career while teaching full time. I spent 12 years at the high school level and 24 at the college level.

I did do some phasing out in the past few years of my career. In 2001, I was diagnosed with Rheumatoid Arthritis. That started to fatigue me at times and it did become more difficult to maintain the energy level and stamina to teach and coach three sports and recruit year round. The first sport I decided to let go of was baseball. That surprised many, including myself. Baseball has always been my passion and still is. Coaching it at the college level is a year-round endeavor. Fall practices, pitchers and catcher workouts in the winter, the regular season [February–May], and recruiting spring and summer. Throw in volleyball, basketball, and teaching; something had to give. I still continue to assist and coach pitchers when I can.

A couple of years later I stopped coaching basketball after 34 years and finished my last two years teaching and coaching women's volleyball.

Three years ago, I got more serious about considering retirement and began to research the possibility. This when the state of Minnesota stepped up.

I was sitting at a retirement seminar listening to all the information provided and the presenter mentioned something called the Annuitant Retirement Program. There was no information in our packets that mentioned this option. After the seminar ended, I stayed to discuss my notes with the presenter to see if I was understanding him correctly, because I couldn't believe what I was hearing. Like the old saying goes, "Not everything that glitters is gold."

This is what he explained to me in a nutshell. First of all, the employee had to request entry into the Annuitant Retirement Program because the state wasn't really openly promoting it. So this is what it boils down to:

X Qualify for the Rule of 90.
X Have a minimum of 10 years of service with the state.
X File a formal request with the Provost.

Here is how it works:

1] Retire and begin receiving a pension.

2] Do not do severance at this time.

3] Come back at up to 2/3 the full-time credit load and work a minimum of two years. Up to Provost if it goes longer.

4] State continues to contribute to Health Insurance and other benefits.

5] At end of program, complete severance package. State buys back sick days accumulated.

6] First year after Annuitant Program state pays salary for last full-time year served again and employee can't work for the state during that year.

I brought this newfound information home to my wife and we continued to look into it. I had to attend a one-on-one session with a Teacher Retirement Association counselor at the MNSCU offices in St. Paul to go over final details and have it explained to me again. It should be noted here that three of the other books I have written are titled: "Random Thoughts of a Stupid Man," "More Random Thoughts of a Stupid Man," and "Still Stupid."

The next step was to bring my wife to the TRA offices and have her review the information and sign off on the paperwork. I asked the counselor why this couldn't be done online or through the mail. He said you have to physically prove you have a wife. I love my wife (married 36 years), but when she was out of the room, I asked the counselor if he was married. He said he was, so I asked him why any-one would fake having a wife and give her his retirement income? He had no answer.

All that said, we signed the paperwork and it was official. I retired in the spring of 2015 and continued to teach and coach for two more years. I started to collect a pension in 2015 and worked at a 2/3 load, so yes, I was making more than when I was a full-time employee.

The severance package was good, and I was paid for the maximum sick days [112] because that is where the state caps it. The money was put into a Health Savings account and pays our insurance premiums. The state got a good deal here; I did not miss a day of work in 36 years, so they got a bargain at 112 days. We also cashed out our TIAA-CREF funds and invested it with Edward Jones.

Now I am being paid my full-time salary from 2014–15, plus the retirement pension, and I cannot work in the state system for one year. I finally got there: more money and less work. Don't judge me; I know you are jealous.

So that question again: "So how do you like retirement?" On paper it looks pretty good for the most part. One detail my wife and I are trying to acclimate to is that the full-time salary for one year is paid in two lump sums, July 1st and January 1st. We are trying to figure it out; tough to adjust after being paid once or twice a month for the past 36 years.

CHAPTER TWO

THE FIRST SUMMER

I have filled my past 35 summers by coaching baseball, running basketball/volleyball camps, recruiting and making sure my incoming freshmen and returners have all their paperwork, and fundraising for the upcoming year.

This summer involved none of those things. I do feel lost not working or assembling a team or preparing for an upcoming season. I do miss the text messages and phone calls from incoming freshmen with all their questions and concerns. I even miss worrying about the academic eligibility of our student-athletes and how they are doing in their summer classes. I did not do any camps this summer and I have not had to make recruiting calls or go watch prospective student-athletes play. I know it sounds crazy when I say this out loud, but I miss these things also.

The typical question has been, "What are you doing with all your free time?" I am pretty sure all I have managed to do so far is replace busy with busier.

In no particular order, this is what I have been doing. Umpiring baseball. Cutting grass at the cabin and home. Working on the cabin with our contractor. The cabin will be our permanent home when we get our house in another town sold. I have also been applying for new coaching jobs. I have turned down a few coaching offers, and I have lost count of how many coaching jobs I have been passed over for. If I had a bigger ego or it was 20 years ago, my confidence would be destroyed. I know I am not done coaching and when the job, location, and timing is right I know something will fall in place. For the time being, I will keep applying and leave it in God's hands to guide my wife and me to our best options.

I did manage to go fishing a couple of times. I have also been able to get some wood cut. Growing tomatoes was a bust; the day I planned to start picking, a doe and her two fawns decided to eat them. For those of you that don't think deer eat tomatoes, I can testify to the contrary. It has been a wet summer so grass cutting and weed whacking has been pretty much a weekly chore at the lake and at home. I have big plans to buy a riding mower in the not-too-distant future.

In between, we have had guests and family at the lake to entertain. I have only traveled out twice this summer. I went to Omaha to see the College World Series in June. This is something I look forward to every year because I also get to see my daughter, her husband, and our grandson. My wife and I went to the cities in late July when our granddaughter was born and spent a few days there.

I have been able to play pickleball on rare occasion. I really enjoy that and hope to be able to attend more in the fall and winter if I am still in the area. I am also looking forward to sleeping in the cabin again. We have had things pretty ripped up with renovations, so I have been sleeping in the bunkhouse since May.

Again, the question: "How are you liking retirement?" I am just not getting the rhythm of retirement yet. Some days I miss the responsibilities of teaching and coaching and other days I appreciate not having to worry about those things and that I have time to do other things. When mid-August rolled around, I felt way out of whack. I kept feeling like there was a void in my schedule and I was waking up early and going to bed late for a few days. Duh! I was supposed to be at volleyball practice according to my body clock. Not going to lie, I got over that and quickly appreciated that I would be able to leave the boat and dock in the water for at least another month. There is definitely a benefit to not coaching volleyball: summer is longer. Again, try not to judge me or question my sanity, but I still miss it. I am trying to come to grips with the fact that I am a coaching junky.

CHAPTER THREE
STILL NO JOB

I continued to apply for coaching jobs throughout the summer and into the fall. Turned down a couple of offers and was denied on several. I am starting to think that being 58 years old, white, not disabled, and not a veteran is a handicap when applying for jobs at colleges. In addition, I am not allowed to work at a Minnesota state college for one year. If I was in the corporate world, I guess you would call this a non-compete clause to my Annuitant Retirement Program.

I guess it was time to own up to the fact that this would be the first fall since 1981 that I would not be employed as a teacher or a coach. I am sure most of my family and friends are questioning my sanity. None of them seem to understand why I am not elated to not be working and why I have not happily embraced retirement.

I have some conversations with people that have been retired for a few or several years and they seem to get it. A couple of them have shared with me that it took them a few years to get into and enjoy retirement. To me it seems simple; if you love what you are doing and you have been doing it a long time, why wouldn't you miss it?

All that said, I began to seek other avenues to fill the void I was experiencing. Tom Coombe became the new head baseball coach at Vermilion Community College and asked me to be his volunteer assistant coach and work with the pitchers. I accepted the position and have been helping with fall practices and scrimmages whenever I can. Ironically, this was part of my initial retirement plan. Ray Podominck, the former VCC baseball coach, and I had planned this same arrangement for the past few years. Ray took a new job at Vermilion campus, but I am glad to be working with Tom as he starts a new adventure in his coaching career. I look forward to helping him. He is letting me work with pitchers, which I have already said I love doing.

I attended VCC in the late 70s and played baseball and basketball there. Over the years, I have wanted to work at VCC, but it never worked out. It is good to be an "Iron man" again.

I still don't own any Vermilion apparel yet, but I'll get to the bookstore one of these days. I will admit, though, it hasn't been a completely easy transition yet to coaching at VCC. I have spent the last 24 years coaching volleyball, basketball, and baseball against the "Iron men and Iron women." It always hurt whenever we lost, and I felt an extreme level of joy when we defeated them. Now I will find joy in any victories for the blue and gold. I think I am already there. We scrimmaged Hibbing CC and swept a double-header. I enjoyed visiting with ex-players and the coaches, but I did quietly relish in the victory.

I have also been officiating high school volleyball. I have 30 matches scheduled this fall. As part of my retirement plan, I started officiating volleyball last year on a limited basis to prepare for a more extensive go at it this year.

I just noticed that in the last paragraph I made reference to my retirement plan. HONESTY CHECK: Truth be told, I really didn't have a retirement plan and I still don't know which colored "Voya" squirrel represents what kind of money. The other thing I have been wondering lately, is what the hell is a Bit Coin? Sorry, I got off track there, but I do have more time to wonder.

If there was a Plan A, I guess I am on to Plan B. If Plan A was to get a new coaching job and end retirement, then I am definitely on to Plan B.

Besides officiating volleyball and assisting with baseball, I have been substitute teaching and doing some paraprofessional work. Two things here; first of all, I am sure I told several people I would never substitute teach and para work was definitely not on my radar. I don't want to do this every day, but I have taken 11 substitute jobs in the first three weeks of school. I have taught English, social studies, 6th grade, and have spent a few days in SPED. I thought that was special education but I have been re-programmed to say SPED. I have enjoyed the experience so far, even though I have been no help to students when they are required to use iPads. The last year that I taught in a high school or junior high we still had film-strips, 16mm film, and ditto machines. Videotapes were just starting to come into use. I am sure that my incompetence on iPads comes as no surprise to my family, friends, or ex-colleagues, players, or students.

I was humbled by a 5th grade student in SPED the first day I substituted. He asked me what I used to do. I told him I was a teacher and coach for 36 years. He responded, "Is that all?" He felt doing only two things for 36 years really wasn't that big of a deal. What do they say about "Out of the mouths of children?"

I am glad I moved on to teaching and coaching in colleges 24 years ago. I really doubt if I would have spent 36 years in public schools. I fear sounding like the old guy here, but it is not the same as it was early in my career. Kids seem to have a lot more problems, issues, etc. . . . Younger faculty seem leery to discipline students. Seems there are more kids dealing with broken homes and tough living circumstances. Definitely more kids on various medications. Two schools I have substituted at have scheduled times during the day for the school nurse to give kids their medications. I have met some great kids though and I marvel at how adept they are with technology and how well some are doing, considering their home life. I'll probably visit these thoughts later in this book. Someone please remind me; my short-term memory is not what it used to be. So, where was I?

So the question begging to be addressed again: "So how do you like retirement?" Still not loving it; right now I feel like I am just dealing.

As things presently stand, I am officiating, substitute teaching, working on projects at the lake, and still doing the groundskeeping at the lake and our home in Hibbing. We still haven't sold the house. The job postings are dwindling on various websites, so I am probably done applying for coaching jobs for a while. Maybe I'll get lucky and something will open up at Vermilion for next year.

I am looking forward to a couple of things, if I am not leaving to take a coaching job out of state. 1] We can expand our Cable TV package at the lake. 2] I can start getting the Mesabi Daily Newspaper delivered at the cabin. 3] My wife and I can travel to Nebraska and Minneapolis to see our kids and grandchildren. I have always enjoyed simple pleasures in life!

CHAPTER FOUR

HANGING IN THERE

I taught a 4th grade class for two days this week. I hadn't been in a 4th grade classroom since I was in 4th grade. I survived!

Despite a big snowstorm yesterday, the kids still wanted to go outside for recess. How great is life when snack time and recess are the highlights of the day? I still have to say I am not a big fan of the iPad. The kids seem to jump to them every time they get a chance. Not very productive, but it does serve as a babysitter. Parents shouldn't be afraid to tell kids to unplug when they get home; they have spent plenty of screen time during their school day. Back to recess. Recess was 15 minutes long, including putting on snowsuits and taking them off. That left about 8 minutes outside. I forgot how much I cherished recess. I think we all did. We should always keep recess in our life.

I can't help but wonder how many retired or out-of-work coaches are substitute teaching? I know Rick Pitino got in a lot of trouble at Louisville recently, but I doubt he is substitute teaching. Who am I kidding? He is probably enjoying the perks of a multi-million-dollar buyout clause in his contract. Then again could he pass a background check to be allowed to substitute teach? I did and they are letting me work with everything from Pre-K to adult students.

One of the 4th grade girls gave me a picture at the end of the day. She drew and colored a picture of a bat flying out of its roost in a tree when the sun came out. We had studied bats in science. We learned that bats are nocturnal and normally returned to their roost when the sun came up. She told me the bat was me and I was flying with the sun up because I should be teaching. She said I was good at it. Made my day! I had never received a picture from a student during my 36-year career. I taught 7–12 and college, so this was a welcomed gesture.

When I'm substitute teaching, I usually end up with some time to kill. For me, that usually means my mind begins to wander. So I thought I'd take the time to write down a few of my thoughts. Who knows if those thoughts will come back. I do own a t-shirt that says, "Have you ever stopped to think and just never started again?"

We do have a buyer for our house. They have put in an offer; the inspection and appraisal went well. The movers (my brother-in-law) are coming later this week and we hope to close later this month. It is not a done deal yet, but we are very close to wrapping it up. It is such a relief to think that we won't have two homes to worry about this winter.

Soon my wife and I will be living at the lake full-time together. This will take some adjusting and working on. Especially for the past year, most of our time at the lake has been spent separately. Since retiring this past spring, I have spent most of my time at the lake. My wife has continued to spend time at home running the Bed & Breakfast. It has been rare when we are at one place or the other together. I will have to start putting the toilet seat down again. We will also have to share the bed again, and I'll probably have to use the outhouse more often. I will also have to wear my headphones when watching games on television. My wife gave me the headphones for Christmas. I will also have to remember to mute my phone and learn to be ultra-quiet when my wife is napping. My wife will have to adjust to me being around a lot more. We haven't spent a lot of time together since I have retired. She will probably encourage me to take more substitute jobs and continue to pursue new coaching jobs. Don't get me wrong, we love each other very much, but I am pretty sure neither one of us is ready for 24/7, 365 days of togetherness and retirement lifestyle. Is anyone really ever ready for that?

Still the question: "How is retirement going?" I'm still going with "It sucks!" but it is getting better. I'm starting to find more things I like about it. For example: last week we went to Minneapolis and Nebraska for a week and got to see our children and grandchildren. We wouldn't have been able to do that the last 36 years. I also like the idea of picking and choosing when I want to work. When I am offered a substitute teaching job, I have the option of accepting or declining the job. Not bad!

Push the breaks! The pending closing on our house has been delayed. My wife and I have spent the past week hauling loads from our house to the lake. We have emptied the house and closed the bed & breakfast business and she is in the process of finishing the final cleaning of the house. We were supposed to close with our buyers this Monday or Tuesday. We have received word that the closing will be delayed indefinitely. The buyers have some issues to work out with their lender. So much for closing before Thanksgiving and moving to the lake and making the cabin our home. Another dream on hold. Hopefully we can close before Christmas. Still sticking to "Retirement Sucks!"

On another note, I worked at a basketball tournament at Vermilion CC the past two days. I worked six games at the scorer's table doing the clock and book. If I ever get back into coaching again, I promise not to holler at the table personnel during games. There is a lot going on there and mistakes can be made. I also want to apologize to any table personnel I may have hollered at in the past when coaching; I feel your pain.

I am looking forward to one of my favorite retirement activities tomorrow. First of all, let it be pointed out that I will go to church in the morning first. Afterwards I plan to watch the Vikings at the Winton Roadhouse and partake in some beer and wings. If you haven't been there yet, I recommend the Captain Morgan's wings. Rich does a great job preparing them. Hopefully I will top off the afternoon by coming out ahead on quarter [25 cents] with the staff and fellow patrons. The weather is supposed to be okay tomorrow, so I should be able to walk the trail through the woods to the Roadhouse. Another simple pleasure at the end of the road in the north woods.

Okay, another perk to being retired. My wife and I were able to leave for the cities on Wednesday to spend the Thanksgiving weekend with our family. In the past, we would have left on Thursday morning or late Wednesday night and returned home on Friday or Thanksgiving night. I have always had to teach on Wednesday and we have had basketball on the weekend. This year we had Wednesday through Saturday. My whole family made it to the cities and we celebrated at my sister's house. Thanksgiving has always been special to our family. My mom always made a point of getting everyone together. This was our second Thanksgiving since my mom passed away. Luckily my sister and her husband have continued hosting the Thanksgiving festivities and everyone made it to the cities to celebrate and spend time with each other. My mom would have loved it. Added bonus, the Vikes beat the Lions!

There was no room at my son's or sister's to stay this year, so my wife and I stayed at a hotel for three nights. (Side note: I am getting tired of writing "my wife and I" so going forward, I will say "Pam" because that is her name. I know, brilliant writing!) It worked out great. We could spend the days with everyone and then escape to the peacefulness of the hotel at night. The beds were comfortable, and I took full advantage of being able to get in a hot tub. We were also able to have our grandson come over and go swimming. Hopefully, this will continue as part of the Thanksgiving tradition in the future.

Another bonus to being able to spend a couple of extra days in the cities was being able to attend the Prep Bowl (Minnesota's High School Football State Championship) at U.S. Bank Stadium. I went to Friday night's game with my son and son-in-law and we watched my cousin's son play for Cloquet. I hadn't been to a Prep Bowl since 1988 and it was my first time to be in U.S. Bank Stadium which will be hosting the Super Bowl at the end of the NFL season. I know I won't be attending the Super Bowl but it was nice to get to see the stadium in person.

All in all, Thanksgiving was a great time and we returned to Ely Saturday night in time to see the holiday parade and the tree lighting in the park. I still want to get to Rockefeller Square during the holidays sometime but right now I'll take Ely, it is great to be home! A complete Thanksgiving weekend, it could have never happened if I was teaching and coaching. Strike this one up as a plus for retirement!

Back to substitute teaching this week. I worked 2nd, 4th, and 6th grade, elementary physical education, and SPED. Very rewarding week and I know for a fact that I enjoyed myself more than Al Franken, Matt Lauer, Roy Moore, Garrison Keillor, or Harvey Weinstein. Who could be next? Hopefully Santa Claus survives the holidays!

Today I substituted for an elementary music teacher. This might be about as far out of my wheelhouse as I can get other than teaching a foreign language or computer technology. I taught second grade and kindergarten music. We were supposed to rehearse the singing of "Rudolph," "Frosty the Snowman," and "Santa Claus is Coming to Town." I am glad that the Christmas program is not for a couple of weeks still, because I probably set the students back at least a week. I hope Mrs. B can coach them back up when she returns tomorrow.

I'm substituting three times this week and four next week; I think that will put me over 30 times since school has started. I assume that when you substitute you are filling in for someone who is not there. In my 36-year career, I never had a substitute teacher; I never missed a day of teaching or coaching. I guess I shouldn't complain—people missing work provide me with part-time employment.

Great news yesterday: Pam and I got word from our Realtor that we have to be in Hibbing on Monday to sign papers on the closing of the sale of our house. The buyers are supposed to sign two days later and we should be done with the sale of our house. I'll believe it when the money is in the bank.

I was all excited today for substituting as an industrial arts teacher. I was hoping to be able to help with wood projects. Turns out all the classes were assigned to study halls or workbook assignments. Made for one very boring day. I guess I wouldn't have wanted me supervising students around heavy machinery either. Probably a good call!

I'm glad high school basketball season has started; it gives me something to do at night. I can go to girls' games to watch my cousin play and do some scouting of prospective recruits in case I land a coaching job at Vermilion or somewhere else for next year. I also go to boys' games because I just enjoy being a fan. Definitely don't have coaching out of my system, and who knows what my future holds for coaching.

Earlier this week winter kicked in and we got hit with high winds, sub-zero temperatures, and some freezing rain and snow. The passenger side door handle broke off my truck when I attempted to open it for Pam; so much for chivalry. I ordered a new one from Waschke's. Hopefully they will call soon to set a time to get it put on. Retired or not, winter sucks! The spring baseball trip to Florida can't come soon enough—only 3+ months to go.

The other day I was substituting at Virginia High School, and the U.S. Women's Olympic Curling team made an appearance at an assembly. Pretty cool. Again, chalk one up for retirement for giving me the opportunity to see them.

Huge week! Pam and I are signing off on the house sale on Monday and the buyers are supposed to sign on Thursday. We can only pray now that everything goes off as planned and the check is in the bank on Thursday afternoon. I can't even begin to describe to you how much Pam, the Realtor, and I have been stressing out the past few weeks. Pam has been a mental and emotional wreck and I have been physically sick for a few days. Anyone who knows me knows I rarely get sick! Hopefully we can end this rollercoaster ride; it seems to change daily whether the buyers are in or out on his deal. I am looking forward to putting this all to rest and getting onto much more pleasant things, like Christmas. We are only two weeks out and we need to be ready for our children and grandchildren who are spending Christmas at the lake with us.

The past couple of days have definitely helped me transition toward Christmas. I have been subbing in elementary schools and you can't help but sense the excitement and anticipation in the younger kids. Christmas art projects, reading Christmas stories and rehearsing for the Christmas music program. Great stuff!

Yesterday I got the door handle on my truck replaced at Ken Waschke's in Virginia. If you have forgotten, I accidentally broke it off last week after we had freezing rain. I also have to have a park assist sensor replaced and to top that off the tank heater on my truck shorted out and burned the cord. Oh, the joys of winter in northern Minnesota just never cease. For those of you not from the north country; a tank/block heater is a necessary device we need to have on our vehicles. If you have to leave a vehicle outside in the winter you plug it into an electric outlet and it heats the fluid in your engine block to keep your engine from freezing up and it makes starting the vehicle easier to start in frigid conditions. I have scheduled these repairs for next week, so no surprise on what my Christmas present will be this year. "On the 13th day of Christmas, my true love gave to me, a park assist sensor and a tank heater for my truck!" Doesn't make for much of a song, but at least my truck will start and I can back up again with no fear. If I'm really good for a few days maybe my wife will throw in some Weather Tec floormats.

When I went to Waschke's I waited in the lobby for an hour and a half. Read a few magazines and had to listen to two men debate who had higher prices, Lossing's Building Center in Babbitt or Voyageuer Lumber in Ely. They also talked about Menard's being much cheaper but getting straight 2x4's was impossible. Seems clear to me, if you are going to get quality products and service stick to the local ma and pa businesses and avoid the big box stores. Definitely worth spending a little more money.

Anyway, as I sat there, I lamented over having to kill a couple of hours waiting but I also realized that I had the time because I'm retired. Chalk another one up for retirement!

So Pam and I signed off on the sale of our house on Monday. The buyers are scheduled for a walk-thru today and are supposed to close with their bank on Thursday. Last night the buyers had more late-hour issues and demands, which we attempted to ignore. This whole thing just keeps getting more stressful by the hour. We are 20 hours from the finish line. The buyers are driving us to the brink. Pam and I have conceded that it is truly in God's hands now.

I am covering a second-grade class all day today. Perfect; they just want to read Christmas books, practice counting money, take spelling tests, and go to recess and the library. Corn dogs and tater tots for lunch and a little quiet time. None of them had questions or concerns about addendums, closing fees, or website domains. Perfect distraction from lamenting and worrying about selling or not selling our house and business. I have never been so thankful to spend a day with 22 seven and eight year olds.

Pay day! It is a done deal; the check is in the bank! The buyers signed the papers on the house this morning. They were a half hour late to the closing, but finally showed up and signed off. Best Christmas present ever! We are blessed. I am really hoping Pam can regain her sanity and health in time to enjoy Christmas with our families. Christmas is in 10 days and we have to get a lot of shopping done and get the house ready for our kids and grandkids. As Tom Farrell always said, "The best lights at Christmas are your kids' headlights when they come home and their taillights when they leave."

CHAPTER FIVE

NOW WHAT?

The holidays are over. Don't get me wrong here, I love the Christmas and New Years' holidays. This year was extra special. Both our kids and their families were here. It was great to spend time with all of them at the lake for a few days. The weather was frigid, but we did get to spend some time outside. It was nice that I did not have to cut the holidays short to coach or recruit. I also got to slip a few days of Pickle Ball in. Definitely not bragging, but I did manage to win my division in a tournament. So, for one day, I was the "King of the Court!" My reign was short-lived, I was humbled by several defeats a few days later. I still have a crown hanging on my dresser mirror as a reminder of my one day at the top of the Ely Pickle Ball world.

The next big event in Ely will be the "Winterfest, the first week of February. I am not going to lie, I have a hard time getting fired up about celebrating winter, but I might as well embrace it because we have a minimum of three months of winter left around here. In northern Minnesota you learn that whether he sees his shadow or not, Groundhog's Day is just a pointless celebration intended for states south of us to celebrate. I do look forward to look forward to seeing the snow sculptures on display in Whiteside Park. If you haven't been to Ely to see the sculptures, put it on your bucket list, they are definitely worth the trek.

The college students are back from the winter break and we have started baseball practice for pitchers and catchers. We won't play a home game in Ely until late April, but this is our version of spring training. All the practices take place in the gym so just use your imagination. We are all motivated by the fact that we will get to go to Florida in early March and play a week of games. I love coaching pitchers. I was a pitcher myself and I get a lot of enjoyment out of coaching and working with pitchers.

I have committed to substitute teaching as many days as a possibly can in January and the first week of February. I am trying to build up my personal savings account before Pam and I leave and take a drive south for a couple of weeks. I can't tell you how excited I am that Pam has agreed to get out of here for a little while. We are planning on going to the cities to see our granddaughter, son and daughter-in-law and then on to Nebraska to see our grandson, daughter and son-in-law. From there we will go to Kansas to see some relatives on my wife's side. After that we are going to just wing it. Oklahoma City, Padre Island, Galveston and follow the Gulf Coast over to the Mobile and Gulf Shores area and work our way home from there. I am not exactly sure why, but Pam wants to work the Alamo in somehow. I'll gladly give her that one, because I want to stop in Metropolis, IL on the way back home. Metropolis is a Superman themed town. Pam also wants to stop in Waco, TX to see Magnolia Farms of "Fixer-Upper" fame. As long as we get to spend a few days in 70-to-80-degree temperatures, I'll take any side trips she wants to make. I am not hard to please, just make sure there is sand, sun and saltwater involved somehow and I am there! We are allowing a minimum of two weeks for the trip. If we have to add a couple of days to that, so be it. Why not, I am retired and Pam doesn't have a Bed & Breakfast to worry about anymore? I just have to be back in time to leave with the VCC baseball team to go to Orlando, FL for the spring trip on March 5th. I know, life is tough!

Super Bowl Lll will be played in Minneapolis next week. I will not be in attendance, have you seen the price of tickets? I will probably be watching at home. I would have gone to the Winton Roadhouse but since the Vikings are out, I think I'll just lay low. Besides, I challenged my friendships at the Roadhouse and wore an Eagle's jersey last week. I don't mind stirring things up for a little personal entertainment on occasion.

I have been asked several times lately by various people if I am doing any writing. I really don't know if this is because they enjoyed my other books or if they want to see if I can redeem myself and write something better than my last book. The first four—"Random Thoughts of a Stupid Man," "More Random Thoughts of a Stupid Man," "Still Stupid," and "A Guide to Middle School and Beyond"—all went over pretty well. My fifth book, "I Still Own a Flip Phone" just didn't cut it, for various reasons. I also know my last book upset a few people. Again, I apologize for that. I can't believe I am going to do this, but I would like to quote Bob Ross here! "Anything that you try and you don't succeed at, if you learn from it, it's not a failure."

So, as you might have noticed the answer to the question of whether I am doing any writing, is yes. I am writing this book and recently I have started writing another book that I hope to get published around the same time as this one. I have become motivated from my substitute teaching experiences to attempt a second book for children. "A Guide to Middle School and Beyond" was intended for pre-teen and teen readers. All my other books have been intended for adult readers. I have enjoyed subbing at all levels, but I have really taken a liking to elementary classes and SPED classes. I have had the pleasure of reading several children's books aloud in classes and listening to students read. I have also gained a deep respect for the work that Paraprofessionals and SPED teachers do. These people do invaluable work in our school systems and are definitely underpaid and their programs are underfunded. Another thing that I have become acutely aware of is the use of iPads in elementary classrooms. Until I started subbing, I was always impressed when I noticed that some schools promote the fact that all of their students have access to iPads. I have seen some very good uses of iPads in classrooms and have become aware of even more misuses or abuses of them. I have witnessed a lot of students wasting time playing games that have nothing to do with the lesson presented or the task they have been assigned. At times I do think some teachers use them as babysitters. Do not think I think they should be taken out of schools; they are a wonderful learning tool when used properly. I just think we need to do a better job of monitoring the use and cutting back on how much time is spent on them.

All that said, the children's book I am working on is titled "5 Days Without iPads." It is a long way from being finished, but I am pretty sure that will be the title I stick with unless the publisher talks me out of it.

It has been eight months now since I officially retired. I still feel I have not completely bought into or embraced retirement, but every day I notice more and more signs that I am a retired person.

Signs of Retirement

1] I wake up and have to spend five minutes to figure out what day it is.

2] My wife is always asking me or telling me what my plan is today.

3] People I encounter are always asking me how retirement is going.

4] When I meet someone new and I tell them I am retired, they seem to automatically assume I have unlimited time on my hands.

5] When I go to a school and sub, I leave right after the last bell and I do not have to correct papers or take notes for tomorrow's lessons.

6] I have taught everything from Pre-K to 12th grade in the last two months.

7] If I drive to Babbitt in the morning to teach, I pass Bob walking his dogs. Bob and I taught together in 1983–84. He obviously has retirement figured out better than me.

8] I keep a personal calendar now. I never did that much when I was working, I just knew I was working every day. My calendar includes refereeing, baseball practices, substitute teaching, radio broadcasting, funerals, doctor appointments, elementary basketball and other miscellaneous events. Miscellaneous seems to be growing.

9] Every once in a while, I wake up and wonder, "What should I do today?" I am starting to like those days.

10] So far, when subbing, I am wondering if I am accomplishing anything. Some days it seems more like babysitting than teaching. One day I broke away from the instructions that had been left for me and we had a class discussion on something the students had written comments on. The students seemed to enjoy it. When I got my evaluation, I was reprimanded for breaking off script and having a class discussion. I still think it was better than just letting them sit there and kill time looking at their phones.

11] A second grader told me the other day, I was the coolest old guy he ever met. I guess that is better than being the creepy old guy!

12] On our computer at home my top four searched sites are 1] Teachers On Call [Checking on subbing openings] 2] NCAA Job Market [searching for job openings] 3] NJCAA.org [checking scores and job openings]] 4] Higher Education Coaching

Jobs [searching job openings].

13] I have noticed when I wake up in the morning my attitude has wavered. For 36 years when I was coaching and teaching, I was always excited and feeling good about the day ahead. Now when I wake up on a day I am subbing, I am just okay about it, the wake-up process is a little slower. I have decided this is the difference between loving what you do and liking what you do. Being passionate about what you do definitely affects your emotional approach to the day. Truth be told, I am also finding that on days I that I don't have anything in particular planned, I feel pretty good and appreciative. If the day has coaching, fishing or a trip to the dump on the schedule I wake up excited and ready to seize the day.

Okay, I don't know if you noticed but I haven't been writing for a while now. The last time I jotted anything down for this book was January 28th.

Today is March 20th, and I am sitting in a classroom in Chisholm, MN bored out of my skull. The teacher I am subbing for today left worksheets for every class or assigned study halls. The classes have been well behaved so I have had time to do a little writing. I think the students are paranoid because I have been sitting at a desk in the front of the room taking handwritten notes. I'm sure they think I am taking notes on them for their regular teacher.

So let's get caught up on a few things. First of all, I am proud to announce that I finished handwriting another book today. So, "Retirement Sucks!" will be my 7th book not my 6th book. Hopefully this weekend I can get the book typed up and sent to the publisher. The book is titled "5 Days Without iPads." It is my first attempt at writing a children's book. I am pretty happy with it and I hope it is well received.

The past month and a half has flown by, lots going on! I went to the cities over Super Bowl weekend. Friday night I watched my son referee the Champlain Park -vs- Park Center boys' basketball game. He does a great job and is quickly moving up the officiating ranks. On Saturday night my son and I went downtown to experience the Pre- Super Bowl madness and go to a Timberwolves game. Been there done that! I don't know what everyone else thought, but I think Minneapolis did a great job hosting the Super Bowl and all the festivities.

Sunday I left early and got home to watch the game. First half at the Roadhouse and second half at home. Congrats to the "Iggles"!

The Winter Festival came and went in Ely. As I said before, loved the snow sculptures in Whiteside Park!

Finally, Pam and I got to get out of Dodge and take our trip down south. It was about 12 degrees below zero when we left and about 83 degrees when we arrived in Galveston, TX a few days later. That alone was worth the drive.

Quick rundown on the trip. That is what you do when you are retired, you give way too much detail when telling people about something you did. Sorry, but I refuse to tell you what we had to eat.

DAY ONE

Drove to the cities. Stayed with our son, daughter-in-law and granddaughter. Pam got to spend time with our granddaughter and I watched our son referee again. I did manage to squeeze in some grandpa time.

DAY TWO

Drove to Nebraska. Stayed with our daughter, son-in-law and grandson. The five of us went out to dinner, Mexican. I had no idea how hot the bottle with the green sauce in it was, couldn't finish my meal.

DAY THREE

Pam and I spent the whole day with our grandson. It was Valentine's Day. In the evening we took him to see the movie "Paddington Bear," while our daughter and son-in-law went out for dinner.

DAY FOUR

Drove to Lyons, KS and had brunch with my wife's relatives. Continued on to Oklahoma City, OK. We got there in time to visit the Federal Building Bombing Memorial and Museum. Very humbling experience, everyone should see it sometime. We stayed at a Bed & Breakfast in Norman, OK.

DAY FIVE

Toured Oklahoma University campus and then drove to Waco, TX. I went to a Baylor baseball game and Pam stayed back at the hotel to plan our day in Waco.

DAY SIX

This was on Pam's bucket list. She is a huge "Fixer-Upper" fan. We went to Magnolia and the silos. Also a lot of antique stores and renovation shops. The highlight of my day was seeing how excited Pam was to be there and going to the Dr. Pepper Museum. We finished our Waco tour by late afternoon and drove to Galveston, TX. I hated driving through Houston. We checked in early enough to walk the boardwalk. It was foggy, but I am sure I saw the beach.

DAY SEVEN

Quick morning walk on the beach and pier, warm but still foggy. Toured a couple of mansions and museums, had a late lunch and headed out of Galveston. We drove to Lake Arthur, LA and stayed at a boutique hotel that used to be an old bank. This was a random stop, but it was great.

DAY EIGHT

Drove to Biloxi/Gulfport, MS. We toured the Jefferson Davis House. Right across from the beach, close enough for me! Drove to Magnolia Springs, AL and checked into the Bed & Breakfast there. Our host got us reservations at the only restaurant in town. Fabulous!

DAY NINE

Spent the day in Gulf Shores, AL at the beach. This was a Mike day, I love Magnolia Springs and Gulf Shores. We got to the "Pink Pony Pub" in Gulf Shores, again a favorite of mine. Met some other people from Minnesota there, go figure! After lunch we drove the Gulf Coast and then headed up to Point Clear and Fairhope So I could show Pam the mansions on Mobile Bay. We had dinner at the Blue Marlin and back to the Bed & Breakfast.

DAY TEN

Back to Pam's bucket list and the HGTV Tour continues, we headed for Laurel, MS. In the morning we stopped at the US Sports Academy in Daphne, AL. I went to Grad School there in 1989-90 and wanted Pam to see it. I also picked up a couple of shirts. We stopped in Columbus, MS and toured the Tennessee Williams boyhood home. After that we drove around the Mississippi University for Women campus. I had applied for a coaching job there and wanted to check it out. I stopped in at the athletic office but nobody was there. Later that day we did a driving tour of historical homes in some town I can't remember the name of. We stopped in Hattiesburg, MS at a renovation salvage store. Pam found some bead board for our house and cut it herself, I loaded it into the truck.

When we finally arrived in Laurel, MS it was early evening. First we drove all over town so Pam plan could get her plan for the next day figured out. We checked in at a hotel and went out to eat downtown. Nice night, great food and outdoor dining.

DAY ELEVEN

All day in Laurel. If you don't know why Laurel, you don't know my wife and you don't know your HGTV shows. Laurel is the backdrop for the show "Hometown." Check it out sometime, the couple on the show live in Laurel. We did it all, the Mercantile Store, the woodshop, various houses that have been on the show, several antique stores and Pearl's Café. Pam actually got to meet the star of the show and her best friend. She was overwhelmed with the whole experience. Don't tell her, but I liked Laurel too. We stayed at a B&B.

DAY TWELVE

More time in Laurel and then we headed north. Stopped in Tupelo for supper. Stayed in a hotel somewhere in Tennessee, just because it was time to stop.

DAY THIRTEEN

Back to my bucket list. We stopped in Metropolis, IL and saw the Superman Museum. I have always wanted to get to Metropolis, the whole town is all about Superman, great stop! Continued north, we ran into bad weather near St. Louis, MO so we stopped at a B&B in St. Charles. Again a random stop, but a wonderful stay. We both really liked wandering around St. Charles.

DAY FOURTEEN

Drove to Columbia, MO. My stop! I also applied for a coaching job at Stephens College. Same plan, seethe college and stop in and talk to someone in the athletic department. Loved the campus, but nobody in their offices. Pam and I went to a Winery in Rocheport and had lunch. We checked into a boutique hotel near the University of Missouri campus called the Tiger Hotel. Toured Columbia's downtown and had dinner at a local brewery.

DAY FIFTEEN

Walked over to Stephens again in the morning, again nobody showed up at their office. On the road again and heading home. We stopped in Austin, MN to have dinner with my sister. This was good, we haven't seen her since Thanksgiving. We finished the drive to the cities and stayed with Blaine and Alex again. More grandma and grandpa time.

DAY SIXTEEN

Home again! Back at the End of the Road!

So, 16 days, over 4,000 miles and my wife and I are not filing for divorce. All in all, a great trip! Seriously, a little random, but a great trip and yes, couldn't have happened if I wasn't retired and Pam was still running or Bed & Breakfast.

My life just keeps getting tougher. We got home on Tuesday and I had to bite the bullet and go back to Florida on Sunday. So, after three days of shoveling and snow blowing and a couple of days of substitute teaching, I went with the Vermilion baseball team on the spring baseball trip to central Florida. I love my life, baseball, palm trees, sun, sand, Waffle House and Golden Corral! Only stress, driving a 12-passenger van full of college baseball players through Orlando traffic.

We have been back from Florida for two weeks now. It is still definitely winter in northern Minnesota, despite the fact that today was the first day of spring. I know some states are considering doing away with daylight savings, I think Minnesota should move the first day of spring to April 20th. It really doesn't matter around here if the sun is directly over the equator today.

Back to the grind, baseball practices in the gym and I have subbed 8 times in the past two weeks. Friday's have become a big deal with Lenten season going full tilt. My wife and I are Methodist but we still look forward to the fish dinners at St. Anthony's Church. Now that I read that back, we sound old. I don't know if it is an old or retired thing, but I can't remember the last time I was up late enough to watch the 10:00 news. Sometimes the 9:00 news on Fox is a push. Any days I sub in elementary classes I never make it to 9:00 P.M. I'd like to say I am getting a straight 8 to 10 hours of sleep but that is not the case. I am sleeping well, but there is that whole get up and pee a couple times a night thing.

I have started applying for coaching jobs again. I really hope I am coaching fulltime by this fall. I am still holding hope that something opens up at Vermilion CC but I can't bank on that. So plan B is applying for coaching jobs and hopefully I can land one. So, if you know of any colleges looking for a 59-year-old, Caucasian, non-veteran, and not disabled coach, let me know. I am not picky, willing to look at head or assistant jobs. Benefits would be nice!

Worst comes to worst, I keep subbing, officiating and volunteer coaching and living the retired life. Not really what I'm hoping for, but it beats greeting at Wal-Mart or asking people "Do you want fries with that?"

Right at this moment my biggest concern is trying to convince some snotty 8th graders that I do know what I am talking about and trying to come up with a good reason for why they should shut-up and listen to me. Thirty more minutes, I can do this.

Rest of the week looks good. Practice tonight and tomorrow. No teaching Wednesday. Teach SPED Thursday and Kindergarten on Friday. Fish fry on Friday. Pam and I might get to Virginia this weekend for the Home Show and some shopping. Hopefully, Duke wins twice and gets to the Final Four. That would definitely help my bracket. I have already lost Kentucky and North Carolina from my Final Four. I still have Villanova and Duke left and Duke picked to win it all.

Stakes are not too high; my total investment is $20.

Life is good, but I'm still not buying into this retirement gig yet!

I also want to share this joke before I forget it. Last week I was at my psychiatrist and she told me that I was addicted to the "hokey pokey." I am proud to say that I have turned myself around! Admit it, you laughed and you will share that joke in the near future. Okay, one more, this one is a riddle. Question: What question can you ask several times a day and get multiple correct answers for? Answer: What did Donald Trump do now?

I'll try not to share anymore jokes throughout the remainder of this book. You can blame the Happy Hour crew at the Roadhouse for those two. I'll admit to telling the first one; Paul is responsible for the second one. With all my substitute teaching, I rarely make happy hour, but when I do get there, my IQ rises or falls several points depending on who shows up.

March Madness came to a close last night and Villanova won another national championship. Didn't change my life much, the pool that I lost cost me $20. The downfall is I will have to listen to Paul and a couple of my relatives gloat about finishing in the money. I guess anyone who managed to win money in this year's NCAA Tournament should be proud. I'm sure Las Vegas loved all the upsets this year. So, not that I was counting on it, but I'll take gambling off the list of ways to make money in retirement.

Today we received more proof that spring is a myth. We woke up to single digit temperatures and a couple inches of fresh snow. If we are going to play any baseball this weekend it will have to be in Iowa. It is nice not being the head coach and trying to get games rescheduled. I'll just wait until Friday and see where I have to drive one of the vans to. For the players' sake I really hope we get to play somewhere soon. Other than our week in Florida, these guys have spent 11 weeks practicing in the gym. To steal a line from the MLB Network, "This is how we Baseball."

As much as I enjoy not having to sweat all the details of head coaching, I miss it and I am continuing to apply for coaching jobs for this fall. I am still hoping something pops up at Vermilion CC, but I still have to keep Plan B in play.

CHAPTER SIX

TAKING INVENTORY

I have been officially retired for about 11 months now. I realize I should have a plan by now, but I have to admit that I really don't. I officially retired last May; here is a quick synopsis of what has happened since.

1] Upon retiring, I received a thank you card and a travel mug from the state. Not sure when they stopped doing gold watches?

2] Umpired high school & legion baseball.

3] Moved to the lake and spent the summer in the bunkhouse because we were working on the house

4] Went back to our Bed & Breakfast once a week to do yard work at cut grass.

5] In June I went to the College World Series in Omaha and stayed with my daughter's family.

6] Our granddaughter was born in July.

7] Started substitute teaching in September, despite saying I wouldn't do that. I have enjoyed it though.

8] Refereed volleyball in the fall.

9] Helped Vermilion with fall baseball.

10] Spent most of the winter attending High school and college basketball games. Kept track of players in case I do get back into coaching.

11] We sold our Bed & Breakfast in mid-December and got all our belongings moved to Winton/Ely.

12] Broadcasted a few basketball games for the local radio station.

13] Our whole family came to the lake for Christmas. Bonus grand parenting time.

14] Continued substitute teaching.

15] A couple of trips to the cities.

16] Pam and I went on a 16-day vacation.

17] I went on Vermilion CC's spring baseball trip to Florida.

18] Play pickle ball every time I get a chance.

19] Have continued to coach baseball, we have been stuck in the gym for five weeks now since returning from Florida.

20] I have been applying for coaching jobs, about 3 per week. No feedback yet.

21] I will start umping high school baseball next week, hopefully?

22] The ice probably won't be off the lake for fishing opener, so those plans are on hold.

23] Looking forward to going to the College World Series in June, might be able to take my grandson to a game this year.

24] I have started looking at zero turn riding lawnmowers. I hope to make that purchase soon, spend a little of that substitute teaching money.

25] Possible summer project? Put a tree-season porch on our house.

26] Main focus right now: Find a coaching job that includes benefits for next fall. Still hoping something opens at Vermilion CC, so I don't have to move out of the area for part of the year.

27] Finished writing my first children's book and I am in the process of getting it ready for the publisher.

I guess this would be a good time to look at the Pros and Cons of retirement as I go forward from here.

PROS

1] Work when I want to.

2] A lot of time at home. [See CONS #5]

3] My wife and I travel when we want to.

4] Get to do all the holidays to do what we want; not cut short by teaching or coaching.

5] More time with family and grandchildren.

6] Time for playing pickle ball.

7] Can be at the lake anytime I want.

CONS

1] Paying 100% for health insurance.

2] Truly feel like I have lost the identity I have had for 36 years, "Coach."

3] Substitute teaching.

4] Volunteer coaching.

5] A lot of time at home. [See PROS #2]

6] Income reduced.

7] Nothing gives me the rush that athletics and coaching do.

8] I really do miss the thrill of competition.

9] People want you to do a lot of things for no pay.

10] I just miss the everyday interactions with student-athletes.

PRO/CON

1] I have written another book and I am still working on this one.

Okay all those things considered, I feel very torn about what is the right thing to do. These thoughts will probably get a little scrambled, but I'll try to explain all my thoughts regarding this dilemma.

Don't get me wrong, there is a lot of things about retirement that I am enjoying. I like the extended time with my family. It is great to be able to go on vacation when we want. It just hit me, do you still call it vacation if you are retired? It is nice to have all the holidays without coaching/teaching cutting into them.

There are several concerns financially, including and most importantly, paying for health insurance. I need to make enough money to continue to pay for the restoration projects we still want to do on our house.

I miss everything about coaching. The players, the fans, opposing coaches, referees, umpires, support staff at games and bus drivers. I miss the camaraderie with all the people I worked with or against. I stay in touch with several of these people but it is just not the same. There are people that still call me "Coach or Coach T," but I don't really feel that identity anymore and I miss it. I don't know if "Retired" is actually an identity, because I really haven't bought into it yet. I feel like I am transitioning to something new in my life, but right now I feel like I am in limbo. Shania Twain has a new song that has a line in the lyrics that goes, "Life is about to get good!" That is how I am feeling, but I wish I could get a grip on what I am really looking for. I have always said there is a huge difference between dreaming and living the dream. Living the dream is much more stressful.

CHAPTER SEVEN
CHANGE OF PLANS

I have always said that "Living the dream" is a lot tougher than dreaming. Take this week for example. Sunday I received word that there will be no coaching jobs opening at Vermilion CC for next year, so that dream isn't happening. Monday I umped four straight baseball games in Duluth at Wade Stadium. More proof that I am truly a "Stupid Man"! If you ever doubted that, read my first three books. I left the house at 6:30 AM and returned home at 12:30 AM. Temperatures were in the upper 20s, low 30s, luckily not much wind coming off the lake. The first game started at 10:00 and the fourth game ended at about 9:45. I can hardly walk today. What the hell was I thinking? I wasn't, I was just "living the dream."

Today the dream continues, I am subbing in a SPED classroom and I am leaving at 4:00 with the Vermilion baseball team. We are playing a doubleheader against Mesabi in Minnetonka tomorrow. This is a home game for us. Maybe we'll play a home game in Ely in a few weeks. I sub in Tower on Thursday and I'll be in Babbitt on Friday. No games in Iowa this weekend, they have snow also. Saturday, I think I'll just crash and burn. Sunday, happy birthday to me! God and the weatherman will dictate next week's schedule.

So, now that I know that Vermilion CC will not have any coaching openings, I can move on to the mythical Plan B. I still am working on Plan A, I applied for a teaching job at Vermilion. Despite my 36 years of teaching that probably won't come to fruition because my Master's degree doesn't quite right with the qualifications but I thought I'd give it a shot.

Plan B would be, continue applying for college coaching jobs. I have applied for jobs in Minnesota, Texas, North Carolina, Ohio, Montana, Kansas, Iowa, Missouri, Florida and Arizona, so who knows where that could end up leading me.

I have been dreaming about a new coaching job, but my wife and I would be faced with a whole new dilemma, depending on location if I get a job offer. Again, "Dreaming" VS "living the Dream."

Breakout day, we finally got outside and played some baseball. First game since we left Florida on March 10th. We split a doubleheader against Mesabi, lost 8–7 and won 8–3. Temperatures in the upper 40s and sunny.

This weekend parts of Minnesota are supposed to see 8 to 10 inches of snow. We should duck it up north. We are hoping to play somewhere in Duluth by next Wednesday.

My so-called relaxing retirement is starting to get a little stressful. I have to try to balance umpiring, coaching and substitute teaching, all based on weather. Again, "Living the dream!" I need to get a real job so I can get my schedule under control.

I applied for more jobs last night, Wichita State, Cochise College and Seward County CC. That is two in Kansas and one in Arizona, all women's basketball assistant coaching positions. I guess they fit Plan B fulltime and benefits.

Other than the fact we got six inches of snow Sunday night, it was a great weekend. I am not going to complain about the snow, the twin cities got over two feet!

Pam surprised me with a weekend get-away to Walker, MN to celebrate my birthday. We met longtime friends in Walker. Bud & Becky Ode drove over from Lake Park to meet us. We visited for a while and Pam and Becky went shopping. Bud and I went to the Portage Brewery, did a little sampling and talked smart. We all met back at the hotel [Chase on the Lake] and had a late lunch. It was great catching up with the Odes, we hadn't seen them for over a year. After lunch, Bud and Becky left and went home. Pam and I stayed overnight. We took in some live music in the hotel lounge that night and ate brunch at the hotel in the morning, before heading home.

As I said, great weekend, except for the snowstorm we drove home in. On the way back, we stopped in Hibbing and went to the movie, "A Miracle Season." It was nice to see a movie, something we did often when we lived in Hibbing. Now, it is a rare occasion because Ely does not have a movie theatre. When we got home, Pam gave me my birthday cake, carrot cake of course!

I really enjoyed visiting with Bud. He gets it, retirement does suck! Bud is going on 75 and has been in a non-retirement phase for about ten years now. He sold his business but continues to dabble in it, consulting and doing sales work. His advice to me was, "If you don't want to be done coaching, then don't stop. Something will work out." So, I will continue applying for coaching jobs and hopefully something will present itself.

I first met Bud in 1981, when I took my first teaching/coaching job in Lake Park, MN. Bud took the job as my assistant basketball coach. I was 21 years old and right out of college, Bud started advising and mentoring me right away on coaching and life in general. He was a true invaluable mentor then and still is. Pam and I have been blessed to have Bud & Becky in our lives and the lives of our two children.

My birthday was my 59th. Nothing special about that, but I really didn't feel like making a big deal of it. The thing I noticed right away, was how much I missed my mom calling me on my birthday. This was my second birthday since her passing. I really do miss her and I miss her calling me on my birthday and telling me about when at what age her brothers died. She would also mention my dad's passing. My dad died at the age of 53 and all but one of her brothers died before that age. I always told her she didn't have anything to worry about. I didn't get that phone call this year but my mom and I still had a moment on Sunday and I am convinced she still worries about me because that is what she does.

The reason I think I am down playing 59 is because I want my 60th year in this life to be a good one. In my demented mind, 60 seems to put you in a whole different category. It is a number that puts you to the older side of the life span. I know it is purely conceptual, but right now in my mind birth to 59 seems a lot different than 60! I guess I'll know next year, hopefully I am blowing this way out of proportion. Birth to 59 has been a fantastic ride; I am hoping 60 to ???? brings its' own set of blessings and good times.

Enough of that stuff, way too deep! Back to "Living the dream." Four days of subbing this week, three more baseball practices in the gym, and possibly six baseball games if we get outside. Also a bonus week, two mornings of pickleball. A little more snow shoveling, but that's hopefully the end of that.

Pam also has reached a new pinnacle in her life this week. She is helping make pasties at the Methodist Church. She has done this before, but this week she got a promotion. Pam has to replace Norm as the potato chopper. Big honor because Norm has done this forever. I know she'll step up and do a great job. They are making over 900 pasties this week, so this volunteer job comes with a lot of pressure. This is nothing to scoff at; pasty sales are the most important revenue producing activity for the Ely United Methodist Church. The Catholics have their fish fries, the Methodist do pasties. Pasty sales take place once a month over a nine-month period and have been going on for well longer than I can remember. A lot of people, in and out of town look forward to the sales.

Winter and spring are still fighting it out. So far, winter is still winning but spring might start a comeback. Fifty-degree temperatures in northern Minnesota by weeks' end. Southern Minnesota still expecting 6 to 8 inches of snow today. Last weekend we ended up with 8 inches and we still have single digit temperatures at night. [Side note: It is the middle of April] Just guessing, but I am pretty sure the groundhog is dead! I am really starting to think I should focus Plan B on jobs in warmer climates. Last night I applied for jobs in North Carolina and Tennessee. If I don't land a new job, I am still getting a refresher lesson in U.S. Geography looking up locations of job openings. I enjoy searching Google Images.

I had a brainstorm last night, thinking about Plan A-. I might approach the Vermilion CC Athletic Director and Provost and see if they would consider taking on an assistant coach for volleyball, women's basketball and baseball for possibly 3 credits each. It wouldn't be full time and no benefits involved. I could continue to supplement our income with substitute teaching, refereeing and umpiring. Sounds good on paper, there has to be a flaw. Okay, decision made, I'll try that and continue with Plan B.

My wife has been working on getting contractor bids for a new porch on our house. We also need to build a new garage and finish remodeling one of our out buildings. There is also a linen cabinet in the hallway, a few more windows and trim and the basement stairs have to be replaced. I don't know about you, but all I see is $$$$$$ when I think about all this. I know we can't get all that done on my pension alone. I need to stay focused on Plan B.

Pam has been working on building her new business. She is running the Zenith which is an "Occasional Sale." She sells vintage furniture and housewares. She has also started selling items online. She is doing a great job of building the business but is still just supplementing our income. I still feel obligated to make the big money! Somehow, I need to make Plan B work.

Right now, I think I will take a break from writing "Retirement Sucks!" I will get back to my notes and the computer and finish typing "Five Days Without iPads" so I can send it off to the publisher.

When I was teaching and coaching, I had a sign on my office door that read: "I have gone to find myself. If I return before I get there, just wait a few minutes. I'll be back!"

Hopefully, when I return to writing this book, I will have good news for you and me. [4/18/18]

[5/7/18] Okay, I'm back. Still nothing huge going on but I have to get some of these thoughts to paper.

The other day at lunch, I was talking to a fellow substitute teacher, let's call her Mrs. D. She is also retired from a 30+ year career of teaching at a community college. Mrs. D has been retired for two years, so she has one year on me. She said she considered going back to college teaching but has decided against it so far. She enjoys not being committed to a fulltime job. I should probably listen to this line of advice more often.

I realize I wrote the "Stupid Man" books but advice like this continues to provide affirmations that I am a "Stupid Man." Why am I not buying into retirement and just enjoying all the perks? It is tearing me up. Larry Mischke has a theory, he says, "God takes care of stupid people."

Now I have three schools of thought to keep pondering:

1] Bud: Don't stop working if you don't feel happy and satisfied not working.

2] Mrs. D: Slow down and smell the roses. Enjoy the fruits of retirement and work when you want to. Avoid committing to fulltime work obligations. Been there done that!

3] Larry Mischke: "God takes care of stupid people."

So far, I would have to say I am leaning toward Bud but Mrs. D makes a valid argument. I hope Coach Mischke is right.

CHAPTER EIGHT

THE JOURNEY CONTINUES

Lately I have been subbing a little bit and umping and coaching a lot. The other day I substituted for a first-grade teacher. One of the little girls in class must have noticed me struggling to get out of one of those one-foot-high chairs intended for first graders to sit in. She looked at me and said, "You know my grandpa says when you get past a certain age there are things you just shouldn't do anymore." I told her that her grandpa was a very smart man. At the end of the day when I walked the kids out to the buses, that same little girl went out of her way to stop and give me a hug and told me to enjoy my weekend. I know we are talking about advice from a first grader, but is this a fourth school of thought I should be pondering?

It was a great weekend, the weather was great, the ice went out on the lake but we lost 3 out of 4 baseball games to Rainy River CC. My wife and I went out and had a nice diner after games 3&4. This is why I know I am not ready to stop coaching. I appreciated the weather, the ice going out and dinner with Pam, but to be honest, losing 3 out of 4 and not playing very well, made for an unsatisfying weekend.

Two weeks ago Pam caved in and let me take her to the ER. She had been extremely sick for a couple of nights prior to that. I can be really stubborn about going to the Doctor, but she takes it to a whole another level. Turns out she had Influenza B. They kept her in the hospital for one night. They did let her out the next day. The Doctor said, "You need to stay home and take care of her, it might take most of the week for her to recover." Side note: [This was the first time I missed a game in any sport as a player or a coach since my sophomore year of high school. I'll do the math for you; that is 43 years. I guess I am bragging, but George Blanda, Cal Ripken, Jim Marshall, and Brett Favre all pale in comparison to that.]

Back to my wife. I know I am not the best caregiver in the world but I did okay cooking, cleaning, shopping, doing laundry, and just overall being supportive in any way I could. I will admit, it was actually nice to be able to take care of her. It is a rarity when she lets me take care of her. I know she is feeling better now and not because of my caregiving necessarily. I just know because she has taken all my newfound chores away; she is giving orders again and is pointing out everything I do wrong. Status quo has been renewed!

Pam's aunt passed away yesterday so she has to take her mom on a trip to Kansas to go to the funeral and visit family. I have to stay back to coach, substitute, and umpire. I know you might be thinking, "What the hell?" Don't be too hard on me; there is not enough time to get my schedule changed. I guess I should be working; retirement didn't make me any more available. Luckily, the week I was taking care of my wife, my schedule was lighter. This is also proof Pam is feeling better and that is a good thing. She is looking forward to the trip and is excited to be able to help her mom again. I will do my part and play the bachelor role for a few days. My father-in-law calls it, "Vacation!"

Pretty embarrassing moment a couple of days ago. I was coaching, sitting on a chair at the end of the dugout. A ball got fouled off above me and our catcher, pitcher and first basemen were chasing it down. I got up to get out of the way, tripped and fell in the dugout. I banged up a couple of ribs and I am still feeling the worse for it. The ribs still hurt but near as bad as my ego. I keep hearing that first-grade girl in the back of my head, "My grandpa says when you get past a certain age, there are things you just shouldn't do anymore."

Just wanted to add this in real quick: A couple of pages ago, if you said, "Who?' when I mentioned George Blanda, Cal Ripken and Jim Marshall, you might be reading the wrong book or you should take the time to Google those three names.

I had a small break through on the job hunt last week. I'm pretty sure I didn't qualify for the Vermilion CC Sociology teaching position. They are done reviewing the applications and I have not heard from them. I figured that, my degree wasn't in Sociology. On the plus side, I did a video interview with Cochise State College in Arizona for an assistant women's basketball coaching position. I thought it went well and I am definitely interested. I hope I get a call back for an on-campus interview sometime this week. Again, I hope Larry Mischke is right.

I still haven't taken the time to finish my children's book, "Five Days Without iPads." Maybe I can finish it while my wife is in Kansas. I have also had six games to ump, four games to coach, and a lot of yardwork to finish at home. Hopefully, I can squeeze in the typing. A couple of rainouts would help the cause. As long as I finish the yard work and make some money umpiring my wife should be a happy camper when she returns. Note to self: Pam will be gone still on Mothers' Day, make sure you pick up a card and hanging plant before she leaves. I think she likes the hanging plants, I get her one every year and she has never said she doesn't like them. I guess you can call it a Mothers' Day tradition.

Things are pretty good right now. Spring has finally sprung in northern Minnesota. I have seen robins and loons, the ice is out on Fall Lake, the DNR has issued a burning ban, temperatures have reached the 60's during the day and we have stayed above freezing for two nights in a row. Vermilion CC has graduation tomorrow and the public schools have three weeks of school left. Our last regular season baseball games are this weekend. Hopefully we can qualify for regional play-offs. I still have several high school games left to ump but only four days of subbing left. Fishing opener is this weekend and the College World Series in Omaha is only five weeks away. Life is pretty good!

It is a good thing I don't have a huge ego or maybe my ego is just very strong. I have probably applied for close to fifty coaching jobs and I have and I have one interview and several rejections to show for it so far. The job search marches on.

Let's back it up. As I was writing this last paragraph, I received a call from Cochise State. I will not be getting an on-campus inter-view, the have decided on another candidate. That one kind of stings. I thought I nailed the video interview. I'll get over it. Again, I hope Coach Mischke's theory is at work.

So, no regional play-offs. We lost 3 out of 4 to Itasca. In the fourth game we had a 10-0 lead and ended up losing15-10. Itasca hit the hell out of the ball and we just ran out of pitching. As the saying goes, "You bring a knife to a gun fight, you lose!" I am sorry to see the season come to a close, I really enjoyed assisting Coach Coombe and working with the team. Great bunch of kids! I'd like to continue assisting multiple sports at Vermilion, but it would also be nice to get paid to do that work. Probably not going to happen, so the job search will continue.

Fishing opener came and went and I still don't have the dock or the boat in yet. Shame because the weather has been fabulous. I did get the tire on the dock fixed yesterday, so hopefully I can get the dock and boat into the water this weekend.

CHAPTER NINE
BACK AT IT

9-5-18

Sorry, but if you haven't noticed, I haven't written anything since May. Retirement got way too busy. Let's get caught up.

First things first, I am sitting in a tenth-grade classroom waiting for class to start. It is the second day of school and I am subbing all week.

Obvious Conclusions

1] I am still retired.

2] I have not obtained a full time coaching job.

3] I have applied for several jobs, interviewed for a few, but no takers.

4] I am trying to finish this book and I have finished another book, "Five Days Without iPads." Still have to turn it over to the publisher. Hopefully Rivershore Books is ready to work with me again.

5] To answer the question, "How is retirement going?" I still haven't fully embraced it, I'm slowly absorbing it.

Summer was good. I went to the College World Series in June. My daughter, son-in-law and grandson attended one game with me on Fathers' Day. That was a special first. I umpired several Legion and VFW baseball games. Both our kids and their families were up for the 4th of July. The fourth of July is always special in Ely, especially when our whole family can be here to share it. In late July I caved in and directed a Pacesetter Basketball camp in Lanesboro, MN. Pam went with me and we had a great time in Lanesboro; biking, tubing on the Root River, dining and we took in a play at the local theatre one night. I do have to be honest here in case Pam reads this book; Pam did the biking, I was not up to it after spending each day at camp. That may not matter to you but I feel better having admitted that. Pam also got to tour and shop while I was at camp.

Pam and I also bought a pontoon boat from a neighbor.

Got a great deal on it. Real happy with this purchase, we have been able to use it several times this summer. On the night of July 4th we were able to take the family out on the lake in the pontoon and watch Ely's fireworks display.

I have done a little fishing, unfortunately nothing to brag about.

Pam and I went to Lake Minnewaska [Glenwood, MN] for our granddaughter's first birthday. Great party, watermelon theme, got a new shirt for the occasion.

In August I participated in a musical production at the college. Those of you who know me, stop laughing! I only had a speaking part, no dancing or singing. I was in Pat and Donna Surface's "Remember When" show. I was a little skeptical at first but I really enjoyed the whole experience. It was all for a great cause. The show was a fundraiser for the "Spiritwood Alzheimer's Foundation."

Pam and I topped off the summer by taking a trip to Nebraska over Labor Day weekend to visit our daughter, son-in-law and grandson. My son-in-law, grandson and I went to a Kansas State football game on Saturday night. Beckett is three and in the midst of potty training so we weren't able to stay for the whole game.

I did have one big personal purchase, a Toro Zero-Turn riding lawnmower. Happy birthday/Father's Day/Anniversary to me! Finally had enough money in my book sales account to buy it.

So that is that and this is now. If you count in school years, this is my second year as a retired teacher/coach.

I think I have a couple of job applications out there that I haven't heard back on yet. I am assuming those will not be resulting in a new job. I am not going to lie, I was hoping to wrap this book up with a bang and announce that I was taking a new coaching job and ending my retirement. Apparently God has another plan for me. God has done a great job guiding my life in the past, so I will trust him to guide this phase of my life also.

So here we go, it is September 6th; it was 30 degrees last night, we had our first fall baseball practice last night and I am on my third day of substitute teaching. I am refereeing my third volleyball match of the year tonight. I am still sleeping in the bunkhouse but I think I'll have to move back into the house pretty soon. I hope my wife is ready for that, she seemed concerned for my wellbeing last night. I told her that the tomato plants didn't freeze, so I am still okay out there.

CHAPTER TEN
TIME FOR SOME AFFIRMATIONS

Okay, first of all, I have to admit that my attempts to find a new full-time coaching position have done some damage to my ego. I have applied for several positions all over the country. Some I thought I was perfectly qualified for and some I realized were a stretch. For whatever reason I have not succeeded in getting any of those jobs. You never get a complete explanation for why not. Usually just an e-mail stating they are moving forward with another candidate. So I am just left to wonder, why? No sense in that, maybe it is time to go boldly forward into retirement. Rick Pitino announced yesterday that he is done coaching. I won't be doing a press conference but I might have to follow suit.

I always said, I don't coach for the money. Now I am definitely going to back up those words. I know I love coaching and teaching kids, so maybe volunteer/part time coaching and substitute teaching is my calling. I also enjoy doing an occasional children's sermon at church. Umpiring and refereeing keeps me in the athletic realm.

Maybe I am qualified for retirement? So what skills do I bring to the table?

1] I love being "Grandpa Mike"! I enjoy and cherish every moment I get to spend with my grandson Beckett [3] and granddaughter Brexley [1]. They are beautiful, healthy and intelligent kids and their parents are doing a great job with them. I hope there are more grandchildren on the way but if not, these two will be just fine.

2] I am starting to get tomato growing figured out. This year's crop was outstanding. I was able to share several with Karl Rukavina.

3] I do an excellent job cutting grass and weed-whacking.

4] I can help with rough carpentry. Demolition, nail pulling and sanding are my specialty.

5] I navigate a pontoon very well.

6] I enjoy recycling and weekly trips to the Fall Lake Transfer Station, burn pile and/or dump.

7] In the fall I still enjoy raking.

8] I win the majority of my quarter bets with Paul at the Winton Roadhouse during Viking's games.

9] I make an excellent pot of morning coffee.

10] I don't know if this is an acquired skill or not, but I seem to be getting very astute at growing toenails and hair in places it doesn't seem to be needed (eyebrows, ears, and back). My wife steps in to help. She cuts toenails and eyebrows and she had me buy a new trimmer for the aforementioned other areas. The back hair is only an issue on hot summer days; the rest of the year she'll just have to look away.

11] I have stepped up my book reading. I actually have a library card now.

12] My computer skills have improved somewhat.

13] My bucket hat collection is growing, much to Pam's chagrin.

14] I decorated the bunkhouse myself. Officially my first man cave.

15] I enjoy and take pride in snow removal.

16] I don't mind using the outhouse.

THINGS TO WORK ON

1] Listening to my wife.

2] Not getting upset when my wife asks, "What is your plan today?"

3] Not rolling my eyes when my wife says, "I have a great idea!"

4] Acting interested in "Dancing with The Stars," "The Bachelor" or "The Bachelorette."

5] Remembering to wear my headphones when watching sports in the living room.

6] Getting out of the house between 11:00 AM to 1:00 PM; Pam's Soapy and naptime. If I get a nap out of the deal, that's great with me.

7] Letting my wife have proper mourning time to absorb "Fixer-Upper" going off the air.

8] Trying to understand why kids at school are so upset with the clamp down on cell phone usage in school this fall. I often leave my cell phone in my truck all day when I am substitute teaching, so I am not that sympathetic. I think France has it right, banning cell phones and other mobile devices in schools.

9] Accepting that my wife is in charge.

10] Understanding when my opinion is actually required.

11] Deciphering "Fake News."

12] Finding new ways to get out of the house.

13] Taking better care of myself.

14] Making enough money to continue covering Health Insurance premiums.

15] Clearing time to travel with my wife.

16] Talking my wife into spending more time down south in the winter.

17] Being as supportive and helpful as possible as Pam continues to deal with ailing parents. My mom and dad have both passed.

18] Finding more time to play pickle ball.

19] Keeping my wife happy. I will always love her and I want her to know that every day.

20] Did I say, listen to my wife?

21] Fishing Fall Lake.

22] Just keep adapting and get better at being retired.

23] I always told my players that the sport they played was not who they were, it was something they do. I have to remember that teaching/coaching was something I did. Now retirement is something I do, not who I am.

I still think "Retirement Sucks," but the next time someone asks, "How is retirement going?" I'll hopefully reply, "It is getting better!"

To quote a line in a movie I can't remember the title of: "Everything will be all right in the end. If everything is not all right, it is not the end."

9-21-2018

My favorite snow sculpture at Ely Winter Festival. I've always liked penguins.

Photo by Mike Turnbull

My son Blaine took me to a Twins' game for a retirement gift.

Photo by Blaine Turnbull

A day at the Pumpkin Patch with Beckett.

Photo by Lexie Baack

Grammy Pammy and Brexley on the lake.

Photo by Mike Turnbull

Snow sculpture Ely Winter festival. My mom loved humming birds.

Photo by Mike Turnbull

Brexley & Beckett on the lake. Can you tell which grandchild enjoys the warmer winter weather in Nebraska?

Photo by Mike Turnbull

Pam's favorite stop on spring vacation 2018.

Photo by Mike Turnbull

Spring vacation 2018. Pam & I posing for our "Everybody Reads the Ely Echo" picture in Metropolis, IL.

Photo by the next guy in line taken on my phone

*Spring vacation 2018. Pam & I overlooking Missouri River
outside of Columbia, MO*

Photo by unknown innocent bystander taken on my phone

Grandpa Mike & Brexley coloring eggs for Easter.

Photo by Alex Turnbull

Another woman taking charge in my life.

Photo by Alex Turnbull

Fathers' Day in Omaha at CWS. Grandpa Mike, Jeff & Beckett Baack.

Photo by Lexie Baack

Grandpa Mike & Beckett first time at CWS together.

Photo by Lexie Baack

Jeff, Lexie, & Beckett at CWS.

Photo by Mike Turnbull

Brexley & Beckett

Photo by Mike Turnbull

Beckett's 3rd birthday. Several superheroes were in attendance.

Photo by Naomi Latourell

Alex, Brexley, & Blaine at 4th of July Parade 2018 in Ely.

Photo by Mike Turnbull

Mike Turnbull

Beckett & Brexley 4th of July Parade 2018
Photo by Mike Turnbull

4th of July picnic at Fall Lake 2018.
Front: Great Grandma Tootsie Loe, Brexley, Beckett, Great Grandpa Rod
Loe
Back: Minne, Jeff, Lexie, Grammy Pammy, Grandpa Mike, Mia, Blaine,
and Alex [New pontoon in background]

Photo by Naomi Latourell

Beckett, Lexie, & Jeff at 4th of July Parade 2018.

Photo by Mike Turnbull

Mike Turnbull

Brexley's 1st birthday. I am wearing my watermelon shirt purchased for the party.

Photo by Alex Turnbull

The Winton Gang; they don't care this is where I park my truck.

Photo by Mike Turnbull

Big day! We got our Mesabi Daily News delivery box.

Photo by Mike Turnbull

"Honey the shitter is full!" This is my annual Christmas picture. It references Clark Griswold in "Christmas Vacation", if you didn't know that already.

Photo by Pam Turnbull

Mike Turnbull

Pickle Ball King for the day!

Photo by Mary Mills

Who are they kidding?

Photo by Mike Turnbull

The night before the Eagles broke Vikings fans' hearts again.

Photo by Mike Turnbull

*Good times at the Winton Roadhouse! Skol Vikes and Fly Eagles Fly!
That is Paul my quarter bet partner in crime.*

Photo by Paul Ivancich

Brexley and Grandpa Mike. I am the one in the bucket hat.

Photo by Alex Turnbull

New mower! Whoever said I wouldn't make any money writing books?

Photo by Mike Turnbull

Mike Turnbull

Blaine, Beckett, and me. We have to get Beckett a bucket hat.

Photo by Pam Turnbull

Boo! [Yes it's me.]

Photo by Pam Turnbull

Gulf Shores, AL spring vacation 2018. I have always loved this place since first going there in 1989.

Photo by Pam Turnbull

Alternative ego?

Photo by Pam Turnbull

Mike Turnbull

Spring baseball with Vermilion CC 2018. I love this job!
Photo by Mike Nelson

Grandpa Mike and Brexley at Rockwood enjoying Tuesday Night Live in Ely.

Photo by Alex Turnbull

Beckett's first day of Pre-school.

Photo by Lexie Baack

Beckett & Jeff at Kansas State football game.

Photo by Mike Turnbull

Grandpa Mike, Brexley, & Grammy Pammy; Easter 2018.

Photo by Alex Turnbull

Fellow Hibbing CC retirees, May 2017. I had to umpire after the party!

Photo by Trent Janezich

Last Hibbing CC Volleyball Alumni game, fall 2016.

Photo by one of the players' moms.

AFTERWORD

If anyone reads this book that is in a position to hire a basketball, volleyball, or baseball coach or assistant athletic director, please contact me. I am starting to enjoy retirement, but I will keep my resume updated.

As I move into retirement and continue to age, I feel I should be wiser and worldlier—not necessarily the case. I have been finding myself more confused, perplexed, and pondering more things in my life. I have noticed that I have begun to develop more pet peeves. I don't remember having too many pet peeves before retiring.

QUESTIONS, PET PEEVES, and OBSERVATIONS

1] Previously mentioned: Why is the hair on my head growing slower and thinner and thriving in areas where it is not wanted? I do have one evolutionary theory pertaining to ear hair and eyebrows. Possibly to filter out things I don't want to hear or see? Nose hairs? I got nothing on that!

2] Do they even sell kids' jeans without pre-manufactured holes already in them? We use to have to play or work hard enough to get holes in our jeans.

3] Do you realize that students in 11th grade and down were not even born when 9/11 occurred?

4] Pet peeve: Empty hand sanitizer dispensers in public spaces.

5] Pet peeve: Pop-up advertisements on computer and phone.

6] Why are newspaper prices going up and the size of the newspapers dwindling?

7] See #6: Same question for snacks at convenience stores.

8] Pet Peeve: People asking me, "Why are you not on Facebook?" or "Did you see [Fill in the blank]'s Tweet or Instagram?" People who know me know I am not a social media user or follower.

9] Pet peeve: People who use Google during trivia contests. Do they not know the joy of having an answer pop into your head hours or days later?

10] Dilemma: I have no problem touching the toes on my right foot, left foot is a struggle most days. Here is the problem, I can cut the toe nails on my right foot and they grow slower. My left foot is out of control. Enter my wife, hopefully she doesn't ever leave me for a long period of time or I will have to get declawed.

11] Why are health insurance premiums tripled for my wife and me as opposed to what would be paid for just single coverage for myself? I would get it if it was doubled.

12] Why did Sports Illustrated send me eight "THIS IS YOUR LAST NOTICE" subscription renewal notices over a year's time?

13] Pet peeve: No water bottle filling stations in a stadium.

14] Pet peeve: Low toilets!

15] One month after I retired, I began to receive a free "Travel & Leisure" magazine out of nowhere. Are you kidding me?

16] Pet peeve: I had this one before retiring. Why don't they ever put a utensil out at a salad bar actually big enough to pick up croutons? I feel bad for all the bus persons who have to waste time sweeping croutons off the floor. Also, I love croutons and I can never get enough.

17] Why does the fall television season start later every year?

18] Will they ever bring back Saturday morning cartoons? I miss them.
19] I have watched the "Today Show" on NBC since I was little. I am seriously considering looking for a morning news show on another network. There is less and less news on the

"Today Show" all the time. The actual news is being bumped by chefs, safety and consumer reports, pop-start, concerts, Twitter posts, etc. . . . I want less of that and more news.

20] Speaking of news, I use to be an avid watcher of the local 10:00 news. Now I find myself checking out Fox News at 9:00 more often. Lately I have been thinking that an 8:00 newscast would be perfect.

21] Do you really have to change oil every 3,000 miles or is that just Valvoline's propaganda to drum up business?

22] I know there is already a bunch of bottled water brands and we have a big problem with plastic bottles that aren't recycled. I am thinking I might start a new business. I will collect empty plastic bottles, fill them with tap water, slap a piece of tape on them and brand them "Tap Water." If it goes well I can expand and add "Outdoor Faucet Water." I'll use plastic grocery bags to bag the bottles six and twelve at a time. I'm thinking 50 cents a bottle, solves a lot of problems.

23] If you take evolution into account, is it possible that humans may eventually have necks like flamingos to adapt to constant cell phone use?

24] I hope I live long enough to see how the whole copper nickel mining issue in northern Minnesota turns out.

25] I truly hope that anyone who was disappointed or upset with my "I Still Own a Flip Phone" book is okay with this one.

26] What a joke! So many major league starting pitchers can't get past 4 or 5 innings that several teams are now using "Openers" instead of a starter. Maybe I should see if I can resurrect my career. I might be able to throw to a couple hitters a game.

27] I find it very ironic that the bulk of my retirement income is coming from two things opposite of what I spent my 36 year career doing. I coached for 36 years, now I referee volleyball and umpire baseball. In my 36 years of teaching and coaching, I never missed a day of work. Now I substitute teach on a regular basis for people missing work.

28] It is fall and the squirrels have started to drop their pine cone bombs from high in the trees. I have only been hit once so far. I love the fall season but squirrels scare me, I am pretty sure they know exactly where they are dropping those pine cone bombs. They have hit my truck several times.

29] Since I am on the topic of wildlife; If any deer read this book, I have three things to tell you. A] The grass is not greener on the other side of the road. B] There is no food in the road. C] Quit teaching your fawns to run out in front of vehicles. It is just bad parenting. They are following your example.

30] Update: I will be an assistant girls' basketball coach at Ely H.S. this winter. I am excited about that.

ABOUT THE AUTHOR

I am a retired teacher/coach. I retired on May 15, 2017 after a 36-year career. Twelve at the high school level with stops at Lake Park, Ely, Norwood-Young America, and Wadena, Minnesota. Twenty-four years at the college level. Four years at Central Lakes College in Brainerd, MN, and twenty years at Hibbing CC in Hibbing, Minnesota.

My wife and I live in Fall Lake Township in northern Minnesota. We have two grown children and two grandchildren. Our daughter and her family live in Nebraska and our son and his family live in Maple Grove, MN.

Pam, my wife, is a retired innkeeper. We owned a Bed & Breakfast in Hibbing for 14 years. She was the CEO and I was the "Charming Groundskeeper."

We are blessed to have come full circle in our lives and have been able to move back to the Ely area. We move forward in this new phase in our lives just trying to find out how we will work it out. Pam is much better at retirement than I am, but I will continue to work at it. She is being very patient with me, and I love her more than ever for that.

BOOKS BY MIKE TURNBULL

* All published by Rivershore Books

RANDOM THOUGHTS OF A STUPID MAN

MORE RANDOM THOUGHTS OF A STUPID MAN

STILL A STUPID MAN

A GUIDE TO MIDDLE SCHOOL & BEYOND

I STILL OWN A FLIP PHONE

FIVE DAYS WITHOUT iPADS

RETIREMENT SUCKS!

Available in e-books and printed versions.

Available at:

www.rivershorebooks.com
www.amazon.com
www.barnesandnoble.com
www.nookpress.com
www.smashwords.com
Zup's Grocery Store in Ely, MN

RIVERSHORE BOOKS

www.rivershorebooks.com
info@rivershorebooks.com
www.facebook.com/rivershore.books
www.twitter.com/rivershorebooks
blog.rivershorebooks.com
forum.rivershorebooks.com

www.ingramcontent.com/pod-product-compliance
Lightning Source LLC
Chambersburg PA
CBHW071454030726
47593CB00003B/1004